THE WATER TEMPLE
Gründerzeit and Jugendstil Public Baths

PHOTOGRAPHS
Dieter Leistner

INTRODUCTION
Annegret Burg

ESSAYS
Hans-Eberhard Hess and Dirk Meyhöfer

Edited by Kristin Feireiss

AD ACADEMY EDITIONS

Cover: Neukölln Municipal Baths, Berlin,
large swimming pool, 1993

First published in Great Britain in 1994 by
ACADEMY EDITIONS
An imprint of Academy Group Ltd

ACADEMY GROUP LTD
42 Leinster Gardens, London W2 3AN
ERNST & SOHN
Mühlenstraße 33/34, 13187 Berlin
Members of the VCH Publishing Group

Translation: Flora Fischer
English language copyright © 1994 Academy Group Ltd
All rights reserved
The entire contents of this publication are copyright and
cannot be reproduced in any manner whatever without
written permission from the publishers.

ISBN 1-85490-387-X

Distributed to the trade in the United States of America
by ST MARTIN'S PRESS
175 Fifth Avenue, New York, NY 10010

Printed and bound in Germany

INTRODUCTION

Annegret Burg

The subject of baths, as described by Dirk Meyhöfer in this book, primarily induces a dream-world. A metaphor for water and for steam, for leisure and for indolence, the subject awakens associations with antique bathing sites that, at the same time, were cultural – for literature, music and philosophy. The bath and bathers have for a long time featured in art, particularly in painting; the theme is embedded in mysticism.

The *Gründerzeit* and *Jugendstil* baths awaken these associations. Their architecture, almost forgotten today, is subtly beautiful and poetic. Its significance is brought back to public awareness by the sensitive series of pictures, taken by the photographer, Dieter Leistner.

Most baths of the Imperial period have been in use up to the present day. However, some remain empty and have been allowed to fall slowly into disuse and decay. Their future is uncertain, due to restoration costs that are considered too high, as well as to the consumer trends of those leading luxurious leisure lifestyles. Consequently, a number of baths are not in use presently, and in other cases, architectural changes are being discussed. Photographic documentation is therefore all the more important, as is the historical and sociopolitical classification of this architectural inheritance, representing a whole epoch in the culture of bathing.

Leistner's photographs transcend the purely documentary approach and are equally far beyond being an anthology of German *Gründerzeit* and *Jugendstil* baths. The actual space, the ornamentation and colouring are the raw materials and starting-point of an original interpretation. Architecture is filtered through the eye of the photographer, oscillating between the matter-of-fact and the poetical.

It is only at a second glance that we discover alienating elements which distort the picture and irritate our awareness. There are departures from strongly visualised realism that occur because of the greater or different objectivity of the camera and of the film material. Because of long exposures, bathers, making tracks in a pool, are transformed into silhouettes, lying inexplicably mist-like in the water. Towels, hoses, buckets – in the picture as if by coincidence – indicate the mysterious presence of bathers that cannot be overlooked. Additional alienation is brought about by diverse sources of light. Film can reproduce types of light – daylight, neon, bulb – in a more differentiated manner than the human eye: daylight is neutral, neon green or blue and the light from a bulb is warm.

The present book is about architecture and photography. The texts – Hans-Eberhard Hess' on photography and Dirk Meyhöfer's on the history of architecture – as well as the pictures by Leistner, relate the subject of *Gründerzeit* and *Jugendstil* baths to aspects of photography, architecture, cultural history and social politics. They forge a link between the culture of the Imperial period and the culture of today.

PIERCING SPACE

Hans-Eberhard Hess

From where do we receive our view of the world? How do we become familiar with the earth's phenomena? In the age of ever-present media and cheap mass tourism this is hardly a question to be asked, even if one is unable to see everything one would like to in the course of a lifetime. We therefore have to rely on exterior information that is, to some extent, second-hand. It is available in books, magazines and newspapers, in films and television and is combined unavoidably with a visual impression, a picture that is usually a photograph.

Without the development of travel photography in the second half of the nineteenth century, foreign lands and their cultural heritage would have remained unknown to many segments of the population for whom travel was impossible at the time. Photographic images of the Great Wall of China, Greek temples, French cathedrals, Egyptian pyramids and Indian religious sites could be seen for the first time. This was the same in the case of landscapes and, more rarely, in that of human beings. Photographs of architecture were not even intended as such. Travel photographers welcomed the architectural motif as the penultimate achievement of the creative potential of a foreign people, proving the existence of ancient cultures. The fact that it was a static historical monument meant that it could hold pace with technical possibilities in the truest sense – the emulsions of the glass sheets that were scarcely sensitive to light and the use of large-format cameras on a tripod with the long exposure time this entails. The first photograph known to us today depicts buildings: Niepce photographed a row of houses from the window of his apartment in Chalon-sur-Saone in 1826.

Architectural photography was not therefore a separate genre from the very beginning. But it is hard to find a name in the history of photography solely noted for architectural scenes until the present day. However, there are several photographers who concentrated on this, alongside advertising and pictures of objects. The Alinari brothers in Florence made a name for themselves in this field in the last century, and developed a lively trade in photographs of landscapes and cities. They created an archive which is still in use today. The 1920s and 1930s were dominated by Constructivism and 'new building'. It was a time ripe for the stylistic development of photography, after the artistically glossed-over portraits of the turn of the century. Bauhaus and Neue Sachlichkeit (The New Sobriety) left their mark. Two photographers could be mentioned in this context: Albert Renger-Patzsch with his clear-sighted observation of industrial landscapes and Werner Mantz who, despite a great love of sober depiction, devoted himself to using graphic details.

Renger-Patzsch was in Essen; Mantz in Cologne. It is necessary to add a third photographer to complete the list. He would have been forgotten were it not for a book devoted to his work which was published in 1982.[1] Hugo Schmölz photographed all buildings by the Cologne architect Wilhelm Riphahn (who influenced the cityscape of the Rhine metropolis more than anyone else) until 1927, afterwards repeating the process with Werner Mantz. Schmölz documented several buildings by the Düsseldorf architect

Emil Fahrenkamp, and interpreted the expressive ecclesiastical buildings constructed by his close friend Dominikus Böhm. It must be understood that a dramatic heightening in Schmölz's photographs could not be avoided.

What, however, is the architectural photographer and how far can he actually go? Should he fulfil the expectations of his client – usually the architect and/or the client? Or should he observe the building like a passer-by, trying to imitate his sense of space? That is providing he is capable of this. German architectural magazines do not exactly provide a forum for the development of photography. Pictures in the monotonous living magazines are often reduced to the optical blob of whipped cream on a product made for the coffee-table.

Klaus Kinold can be counted among the few photographers who counteract what has become a parody of architectural photography, 'I want to show architecture as it is. Architectural photography entails showing what you see. I do not aim to manipulate. I do not wish to conjure up a certain atmosphere. I do not use artificial light and do not search for light effects. I also do not wait for a sensational position of the sun or the light in order to create drama. I avoid all of that. I actually wish to show the building in the way it is seen by the observer for twelve hours of the day.'[2] Therefore Kinold, the purist, even rejects colour in photography, 'While the tones in black-and-white photography are seen as an abstract conversion, rather from the point of view of a differentiation of tones (therefore of the differentiation and demarcation of depicted objects and of an aesthetically pleasing reproduction), the colours in colour photography are accepted by the observer all too easily as being "realistic". Just as one can see past reality, one can photograph past architecture. This takes place more easily with colour photography.'[3]

This is a point of view that can be respected. It is actually also highly convincing. However, there is another contemporary architectural photographer who has completely dedicated himself to colour – Dieter Leistner. Kinold at least takes into account the colour photographs of the Italian, Luigi Ghirri (his fellow countryman, Olivo Barbieri, should also be mentioned). But it was Leistner who introduced colour into architectural photography – at least in interior shots where this had previously not existed because it was too difficult to manage. According to Leistner, a house 'is a living organism' and therefore he does not hesitate in photographing it as it appears. Leistner has to a certain degree made architectural photography socially acceptable. It can be reproduced in the majority of magazines that print in colour.

However, it did not originally seem likely that Leistner would become a photographer. He was born in 1952 in Steinlah, Lower Saxony. Initially he learnt carpentry, a trade he practised for over seven years in Lower Saxony and Saarland. It was only his second educational choice that made a photographic training possible: several semesters of photographic engineering in Cologne, in the department of visual communication at the Folkwangschalle (today the Gesamthochschule of the University of Essen) and communication design in Wuppertal. He stubbornly fought for these possibilities. This helped him, then as now, to assert his own ideas during the realisation of his commissions ...

Leistner is additionally searching for the practical side of photography. His finger exercises are lyrically enchanting landscape photographs – for example, trees in the fog. Therefore the important conclusion must be reached that what the pictures portray was difficult to achieve. This is an experience not unknown to craftsmen: the attainment of technical maturity, the process of working, comes before the result. He soon learnt to think conceptually. His first project took place in Essen. He photographed tram stops with their shelters and billboards frontally. These are pictures that communicate part of the history of the Ruhr.

One of the guest lecturers in Essen was Reinhart Wolf who died in 1988. He was probably the best-known German advertising photographer in the field of still-life. He achieved respect and a high degree of recognition in the applied photographic field. Wolf also cultivated architectural photography in colour. This began with the white, wooden farmhouses of Georgia in the United States, continued with the brick architecture of northern Germany and culminated in the famous skyscraper towers of New York for which Wolf created a photographic monument. He later made a great impression with his Spanish castles, dipped in the warm light of the South.[4] When Wolf asked the student Leistner, what he would photograph next, he answered spontaneously, 'Old swimming baths'. Wolf advised him to carry this out, and if not, he would do so himself. It is possible that Leistner's regular visits to the baths in the Deutz area of Cologne provided the inspiration for this idea.

He therefore executed what would become his diploma task from 1980 to 1982: photographs of the German swimming baths of the *Gründerzeit* and *Jugendstil*. The concept envisaged making comparisons between the architecture of the baths of various cities, at the same time as depicting the pleasures of swimming. Thus reasons, Leistner always chose similar standpoints from which to photograph, as well as the same focal length. Swimming baths present a maximum amount of information and were usually designed as centrally structured buildings. Leistner's camera was therefore placed at the narrow edge of the basin and the photographs taken on the diving board or away from this to the other wall of the building. In order to curtail the loss of detail as much as possible, he used the large, professional camera with a negative format of 8×10 inches, roughly corresponding to the size of a DIN A4-size page. Leistner does not, however, prettify what he sees. He does not arrange, rearrange or tidy up anything. The viewer is meant to realise that the baths are in use. Therefore, the rubber hose can wind around the edge of the basin, while the swimming teacher's lassoo or tools stand around. On closer examination, the viewer realises that a swimmer must recently have been in the pool because of the irregular surface of the water. It is unfortunately not possible to remove this, as the open camera shutter with its long exposure time has simply swallowed it up.

In contrast to black-and-white photography, light in colour photography can be problematic. The film records the diverse sources of light (halogen, neon, lightbulbs, etc) more precisely than the human eye. The photographer will never be able to reproduce a so-called 'neutral' impression of an image. This does not cause great difficulty with swimming baths, as they have a high degree of daylight. But as soon as artificial light is added, it is necessary to filter out colours that seem 'unnatural'. However, this is a dictate to which Leistner is unwilling to succumb. Contrary to this, he lets the shrill colours of fluorescent tubes glow on purpose. He fills spaces with types of light that, although they exist, can not be recorded by the naked eye.

Leistner is not attempting to find the 'right' light or to expose at the 'right' moment (which already exists in documentary photography – according to Cartier-Bresson). He does, however, know how to correct, chance or add to existing light sources if certain effects are to be achieved. In this case, the problem is that of photographing against a large window as a background – every photographer's nightmare, even today.

Light only creates space in a two-dimensional image. In Leistner's experience, it is difficult for architects to understand that a photograph is not a house and that it is light that delineates a building and a space and makes recording it possible; providing the viewer with an impression of architecture. Diffused light, ideal for black-and-white photography – differentiating shades of grey by a clean division of tones and leaving behind a complete aesthetic impression – can appear boring in colour photography and can bring about a loss of orientation. The photograph becomes coincidental and beautiful only coincidentally.

Architects have long been able to trust architectural photographers; they know that Leistner can fulfil their intentions. Some create their characteristic forms – squares, circular segments, ellipses, round shapes – and therefore he also takes 'round' pictures. He will then follow right-angled corners, if the building style is square and right-angled. Gottfried Böhm and OM Ungers, for example, allow their work to be interpreted mainly by Leistner. His architectural photography is in demand – whether as documentation for architects or building clients in the form of brochures, for magazines, or for the design of advertisements and calendars. This is less because of his style, as far as one can even speak of this in the field, but more because of his self-conscious treatment of architecture. Photography now has a solid base, so that nowadays it is possible to speak of the existence of architectural photographers. Leistner also provides a profound training for future generations as a teacher.

The series of photographs of baths, originally conceived as a diploma task, has been published in many magazines: *Art, Casa Vogue, Color Foto, FAZ-Magazin, Photo Technik International, Zodiak,* etc. Dieter Leistner has amended and updated it for this book. He includes Augsburg, Berlin-Neukölln, Nüremberg and the now more accessible part of Germany – Berlin Prenzlauer Berg, Dessau, Halle, Leipzig and Jena. As can be seen, Dieter Leistner is a perfectionist.

1 Karl-Hugo Schmölz and Rolf Sachsse; *Hugo Schmölz, Fotografierte Architektur 1924–1937* (Architecture in Photographs 1924–1937), Mahnert-Lueg Verlag, Munich, 1982.
2 Ulrich Weisner (Editor); 'Ich will Architektur zeigen wie sie wirklich ist' ('I want to show architecture as it really is.') *Klaus Kinold, Fotograf.* Exhibition catalogue, Kunsthalle Bielefeld, 1993, p18.
3 Op cit, 2, p33.
4 Hans-Eberhard Hess; *Reinhart Wolf,* Verlag Ellert and Richter, Hamburg, 1992.

PUBLIC SWIMMING BATHS
A BUILDING TYPE OF THE
SECOND GERMAN KAISERZEIT

Dirk Meyhöfer

Dedicated to my father, Gerd Meyhöfer, who developed a very different type of 'bath' in order to meet the demands of a leisure and consumer society.

The subject of baths is seductive. As Louis Aragon[1] has already surmised, 'We are somehow convinced that there is a close connection between baths and desire and that there is indeed an ancient belief that enhances the secrets of these public amenities.' Every culture up until the present, whether antique, Oriental or Japanese, has manifested itself with the construction of thermal baths and bathing houses. On leafing through this volume of pictures, one quickly senses what can be referred to as a sense of well-being. The photographs are highly nostalgic and harmoniously beautiful. One feels this despite the fact that Dieter Leistner always attempts to take photographs that are 'objective and true to nature', and without resorting to the soft-focusing lens and similar tricks.[2]

Appearances can be deceptive. From the first pages, it will become obvious how the social history of the bath, that begins at this point, leads deep into the turbulent history of the second German Imperial period. The term 'public baths' (the English equivalent of the German term *Volksbad*) emerges and will prove to be the underlying theme of this study. It is a term which suggests connotations of class solidarity that were not, however, to be achieved. Instead, the most important function of these highly familiar architectural gems was to discipline the Imperial Navy.

This is hardly surprising. Johannes Roth wrote an appropriate and poetical essay in the *Frankfurter Allgemeine Magazin*[3] in which he concentrated on Greek antiquity and its bathing delights. He admitted that 'Greek warriors had to be able to swim, otherwise Themistocles would not have been able to win the Battle of Salamis.' In other respects, too, the Greek period was similar to that of Wilhelm II – for on the whole, it was the upper classes who could swim; those who could neither write, read, nor swim were considered plebeian by the Athenians.

1. LOOKING BACK: A SHORT OUTLINE
OF THE HISTORY OF BATHING

One of the pioneers of the modern architectural movement, the Swiss Siegfried Giedion, organised the exhibition 'The Bath – Past and Present' for the Museum of Applied Arts in Zürich in 1935.[4] In an edition of 'weiterbauen', a supplement of the noteworthy *Schweizer Bauzeitschrift* (Swiss Building Magazine), Giedion concluded precisely how antique culture had already thoroughly mastered bathing and had expressed this architecturally, 'The bath can be understood from the point of view of the "cultural whole". The bath, consisting of periodic pouring of water and showers, occupied a relatively small space in

11

the Greek gymnasium. It was enmeshed, however, in the whole physical and spiritual education programme of the gymnasium, eventually becoming a social centre in Roman culture. The ground plans of Roman spas took over individual details of the gymnasium and at the same time expanded the idea of bathing. Bathing became a complex process. It was recognised that the ordinary bath was insufficient for recuperation, as the human body can only recuperate with increased blood circulation and gland activity. This summarises the function of the steam bath, the fundamental element of the Roman bath; several rooms of varying temperatures (up to seventy degrees Celsius) for increasing the body temperature were entered.'[5]

From Roman baths to the medieval bathing parlour

The culture of bathing reached the furthest corners of Europe (the British Isles, for example) as well as Asia Minor and North Africa, due to the increasing power of the Roman empire. Giedion also believed that Islam found the inspiration for its own bathing culture in Rome.[6] The magnificent Roman buildings erected by Diocletian and Caracalla are examples of a bathing culture that outshone the bathing customs of the Sumerians, the Assyrians and naturally also those of the Germanic tribes. Following the decline of the Roman empire, there 'were no marked changes in European bathing customs for hundreds of years.'[7] A noteworthy change did not occur until the eleventh century when the Crusaders came into contact with oriental bathing rites, that can be understood, in fact, as a development from their own (Roman) history. It should also be mentioned that medieval 'bathing parlours', were intended as refuges from leprosy and other infectious diseases. The bath soon developed from being simply a hygienic facility into becoming a favourite meeting-place in urban life in the medieval city. There are obvious parallels to the late nineteenth century, as diverse modes of bathing applied to the various social levels. The actual bathing procedure began with cleansing. 'Poorer people,' Horst Prignitz differentiated, 'poured water over themselves, while rich guests let themselves be washed with soapy water by the bathing master. After ending the cleansing process, sometimes also combined with a massage, one proceeded to sweat. This was the most important part of the bath.'[8] Prignitz followed this with a description of a process that has much in common with what is described today as taking a sauna.

Those who drew blood in order to prevent disease were as at home here as those who cut hair and shaved the public. People involved in the construction of buildings had their topping-out ceremonies here. They ate and drank. An enormous tiled stove inside made the bathing parlour one of the few warm places in the town. It therefore took on a function comparable with that still existing in small Finnish villages and became a centre of social life. Consequently, Finnish saunas are places for both birth and death.

The medieval bathing parlour was not a defined building type. It did not need a considerable amount of space, was integrated into the houses of ordinary citizens, and was built optimally on pieces of land near fountains, canals or streams. With the waning of the Middle Ages and the onset of the Reformation and Counter-Reformation, an all-time low in matters of the body was reached. As Giedion wrote, 'This was reached in the seventeenth and eighteenth centuries. The warm bath became merely a place of luxury and eroticism.'[9]

Health resorts were developed in Central Europe (mainly in Bohemia) and later in Britain where seaside resorts such as Brighton became fashionable. Those on the Baltic Sea – Heiligendamm or Putbus – soon followed. They were highly important in cultural history and were frequented by the aristocracy, and by most of the upper class. Citing the example of Schwalbach in Hessen, Matthäus Merian described this in his *Topographica Germanica* as follows, 'After the Thirty Years War, Schwalbach became the most highly frequented luxury bath in Germany. Sometimes as many as thirty tables would stand in the large gaming room: exciting balls, hunts, rifle shooting and outings were some of the pastimes of this elevated section of the public. Only the aristocracy was permitted to dance at the balls, while the middle class had to stand behind the chairs. Jewish visitors had their own position at the well. It was forbidden for them to draw water themselves and they had to remain fourteen steps away from the well.'

The Enlightenment and, above all, the first hectic effects of industrialisation, brought with them a radical change of ideas. Figures of the Enlightenment such as the philosopher Jean Jacques Rousseau, the doctor Ludwig Jahn or the pedagogue Johann Christoph Friedrich Guts Muths, soon recognised the importance of a healthy population, physical training and discipline. A movement that had begun in England, where European industrialisation had first taken place, soon reached Germany. The movement of the population from the country to the increasingly makeshift towns, resulted in uncontrollable growth ('the removal of refuse is especially problematic!'[10]) and soon led to chaos – perhaps comparable only to contemporary squatter areas in Cairo or Rio de Janeiro. Radical re-thinking took place in England (around 1831) after the heavy cholera epidemics.

For the first time laws decreed sewer construction, the availability of water and 'public housing' on a larger scale.[11] Barbara Hartmann explained accurately in an outline of the history of bathing[12] that the 'construction of baths belonged to the sphere of socially hygienic measures, catering for urban hygiene and the prevention of epidemics', which thereby indirectly recalled similar medieval processes.

It is hardly surprising that it was the rich port and trade city of Liverpool that introduced the first public washing facilities.[13] Those with bathtubs and wash-stands followed in 1842 in Liverpool, and in 1845 in the London Docks. Following the Sir Henry Dukingfield Act in 1846, the construction of baths became a municipal, and therefore also a social, task.[14]

At approximately the same time as ten such facilities, or so, were in operation in London, public baths were erected in Berlin and Hamburg, the two German towns that could be termed metropolises. Once again the establishments here were the direct result of a cholera epidemic.

An early example:
Washing and Bathing Centre at the
Schweinemarkt in Hamburg

This facility was one of the most interesting 'baths' in this phase of reorientation, designed by the British engineer William Lindley – who was later to build Hamburg's progressive sewer system. The conspicuous, round, centrally constructed building erected solely in brick was simply plastered with Portland cement on its front in its early years. As can be seen, great lengths were not always taken, as would be the case with the customarily white residential and communal buildings. Baths were of minor importance. The construction of a public water supply was necessary to make the new bathing facilities even technically possible. 'This was founded in 1854, at the behest of the Patriotic Company, by a joint-stock company and was found at the highest point of the old city, enabling flushing and ventilation of the sewers.'[15] Hamburg was provided with a rather droll building for a little over 68,000 Taler. A circular building (which fell into decay after World War II) surrounded the central, yellow brick chimney in the manner of a circus tent. The inner circle enclosed wash-stands, while the outer – following the British example – had separate bathtubs for men and women: 98,089 baths were taken by men and 24,305 by women in 1867.[16] This was a discrepancy that would soon find a concrete echo in the dimensions of female swimming baths, which were smaller than those of the males in most public baths.

2. PUBLIC BATHS: THE EMERGENCE OF A NEW TYPE OF BATHING INSTITUTION

Washing and bathing facilities were the precursors of 'public swimming baths'. From the earliest adaptations of 'English' baths, in about the middle of the nineteenth century, until the culmination of the bath building boom at the beginning of the twentieth century, designs were discussed and ideas polished. Developments increased faster after the founding of the German *Reich* in 1871, which was actually the first period termed the *Gründerzeit*. Up until then, there were only hygienic facilities to speak of; there were practically no swimming pools in existence. Even after the *Reich* was founded their function changed little, as is illustrated by the term frequently used – 'public shower'. However, these changes were regarded as a public necessity as were improvements in living conditions, particularly for the working class.

Public showers versus regenerating baths

It was perhaps for these reasons, as well as because the time was right, that the first large swimming pool was built in Bremen, in 1877 (men such as the priest Kneipp, or the *Turnvater* – 'father of gymnastics' – Jahn, had discovered the great importance of sports for public health). A breakthrough was achieved in the 1880s when double the number of baths were constructed than in the preceding thirty years.[17]

A synthesis of two diverging concepts – represented by those of the DGV, the German Society for Public Bathing (developed from the Berlin Society for Public Bathing, today called the Bathing Society) and those of the Berlin dermatologist and first chairman, Oscar Lassar – was responsible for further developments.

This variant must be described as a 'minimal solution', but one that seemed fitting in view of the ever increasing hygienic problems. 'Every attempt at ameliorating our poverty in matters of bathing must be welcomed joyfully. However, one is less concerned about decorating several particularly favourable areas with pleasing facilities. The fundamental principle is established: a weekly bath for every German! At first, only the most simple means imaginable could be achieved. The lukewarm shower must be placed in this category. Here one can see the form of bathing in the future.'[18] Writing in 1887, Lassar revealed that he was close to reality. His system of cheap showers, housed in tin pavilions, as shown at the 1883 World Hygiene Congress in Vienna, was of military origin.[19] 'The underlying concept, in this case, comes from our army. The general practitioner, Dr Münnich, who is sadly deceased, had constructed a collective shower for the bathing of the troops at the local Emperor Franz Grenadier Kaserne Barracks.'[20]

Lassar, who was highly socially conscious, employed the same degree of energy in the construction of public showers as he employed to reject its alternative – the so-called regenerating bath. Although he also believed that 'the bath belonged to those forms of good living that one should grant all classes of society and actually develop',[21] he also warned about 'overloading resources too heavily.' In other words, Lassar the doctor regarded swimming pools as being superfluous and ineffective.

Although the regenerative bath, with its swimming pool and hot air baths, finally took over from simple showers (a list dating from 1902 already cites over 150 German cities that had baths with swimming pools),[22] this had less to do with Lassar's opponents, such as Leo Vetter, who stressed the recuperative qualities of swimming pools in the spirit of Jahn, than with the realisation that public baths, under municipal administration since the 1890s, could be run more profitably.

These financial considerations made opponents' arguments, like those of the Danzig Governmental Councillor of Medicine, Dr Borntraeger, appear superfluous, 'At long last, swimming pools can no longer be considered completely safe. One can imagine being wounded, even killed, by falling, drowning or catching infections in the communally used water; these are undeniable facts.'[23]

In conclusion, if it is today possible to consider 'public baths', where Dieter Leistner has been able to take photographs of the huge pools, then one can only thank those with the power to make decisions in the society of that time. They realised that not only had the state of hygiene to be improved, but also that medical, military, economic, socially reformatory and ethical-moral aims had to be pursued.[24] Public baths belonged to a strategy that attempted to counteract the breakdown of morality, the destruction of peace and order and the fact that a whole section of society could become brutalised. This may sound rather flippant but it is an element that actually touches the centre of the reorganisation of society in the Imperial period (and precisely because these conflicts were not solved, catastrophes and the decline of the Empire later occurred). The sociologist, Wolfgang R Krabbe, summarised this situation as follows, 'We are concerned with a movement that tried to deal with the social problems of its day in its own particular fashion. It developed accompanying designs for programmes that should lead to evolutionary changes in society which would be realised by the sum-total of individual, auto-didactic education.'[25]

Public swimming baths without a public?

Those who check the validity of this thesis about baths that have been constructed, who analyse the ground plans or compare the entrance prices, will recognise that it does not apply in the case of public baths.

The term itself creates confusion. The public, as a whole, was not welcome in the swimming pools of that era; at least, not all at once, or not in the same pool. Lassar and his friends in the DGV undoubtedly considered that the working classes had priority. This did not happen without protest. A county secretary for insurance from Danzig, named Geppert, contradicts this in 1904: 'I define the people, in accordance with a generally held belief, as the great mass of the middle class, as opposed to the upper class that dominates, due to political influence, wealth and education.'[26]

If, however, the middle class ever went bathing, then it was never in the company of the working class. That was considered improper. It was similarly indecent for gentlemen to swim in the same pool as women or school-children. This led to discriminatory guidelines. The monthly, *Die Frau* (Woman),[27] complained in 1907 that 'while male working hours are taken into consideration, the opening hours for women were only from 9.30am to 12pm and from 2pm to 4pm. How could a working woman go bathing? What should women who work at home do?' Where such perfidious opening hours were insufficient, entrance fee policies were imposed. This worked on two levels. In Müller's Public Baths in Munich at the turn of the century, for example, the working class was indirectly excluded by the entrance fee of 40 Pfennigs (the hourly wage of a Berlin worker, paid by hour, not at piece rates, was forty-five Pfennigs)[28] because they could, and wanted to spend only a Groschen on bathing. The entrance fee of ten Pfennigs applied only on Saturdays and to the days before holidays after 5pm when the bourgeoisie followed other pursuits.[29]

In some cases, two male swimming pools were affordable at the same time, as at the Goseriede Baths in Hanover – it was open at all times for 'those of lowest means'.[30] However, it had fewer facilities: '22.5 metres long, 10.6 metres wide, with 240 square metres of water surface and 330 cubic metres content; the Male Pool 1 was 14 metres wide and 28.50 metres long, therefore comprising a water surface of 404 square metres and a volume of 659 cubic metres of water!'[31] This is a discrepancy that becomes more obvious when it is realised that 'mass lessons for school children' took place in the smaller, rather than the larger, pool. There was also a separate entrance with 'ten Pfennig machines', leading to the *Armenhalle* (pool for the poor).

Public baths can not be regarded therefore as places for everyone under one roof, where diverse classes and groups of the Empire could meet in a conciliatory manner.

Concerning railway stations, arcades and public baths

These had important effects on the design of ground plans and the planning of space. The result was usually a Janus-faced complex. The building was structured symmetrically, as separate male and female bathing areas were prerequisites.[32] This basic, symmetrical ground plan was rejected from time to time when parcels of land were irregular (as was the case of the Elisabeth Baths in Aachen). This division into two areas was soon insufficient for the social demands in many cities. Additionally, bathers were separated according to 'rich and poor', following the motto, 'the poor in the cellar, the rich on the first floor.' A third pool was therefore available.

Furthermore, as the problem of constructing 'public baths' was a new phenomenon, models or influences did not actually exist. Abroad (for example, in London or Paris), several baths had been built which were reminiscent of Islamic hammams or Roman baths in decoration and shape, due to a more restricted cultural interweaving in the first half of the nineteenth century. However, these appeared unsuitable for modern facilities which combined baths for washing and swimming. (There are several exceptions, mainly in the sphere of luxury and thermal baths; the Thermae Novae in Badenweiler clearly followed the example of the thermal baths of the historical frigidarium.)

As for the characteristic architectural strengths of the nineteenth century, these are reflected in the small baths in Hamburg, constructed in 1854 whose 'style was determined by Greek and Gothic elements'[33] as the historians who specialise in this century – such as Leonardo Benevolo or Claude Mignot – like to prove. Mignot writes that 'architecture is original when it is contradictory and experimental';[34] another of his ideas – that industrialisation, as well as the discovery of new building materials this brought with it, gives building new impulses – shows how this small building related to the *Zeitgeist*, with its romantic chimney, and yet was greatly reminiscent of antiquity. This bathing institution in Hamburg, however, did not become an example of a building type. It could not be so, for baths were never influential buildings in the nineteenth century.

In considering the newly constructed and most characteristic buildings of the nineteenth century today, galleries, arcades and department stores come first to mind and then railway stations. Jean Dethier aptly terms them 'temples of technology',[35] as they consciously referred again and again to the daring heights of medieval church naves. Another reason, was that only railway stations were permitted to dominate the cityscape with towers. Undoubtedly the most impressive arcade is the Vittorio Emanuele II arcade in Milan. Johann Friedrich Geist regards it as an 'arcade in the manner of Roman baths and the worldly counterpart of the cathedral.'[36] Those who have crossed the 197 metres length or the 105 metres width, with a maximum height of 47 metres, will understand what he means. There is an apt quotation by Cendrars concerning the new railway stations – he describes them as 'the most beautiful churches in the world'.[37] The nineteenth century invented the railway and an open form of trade, crossing national boundaries, had only become possible after the French Revolution. It is hardly surprising, therefore, that railway stations and department stores are considered the true monuments of architectural culture in the nineteenth century.

The consistency of form of both types of building was defined *a priori* by function. For example, high railway halls were necessary in the age of the steam locomotive in order to provide a more efficient disposal of smoke. Besides, railway stations and department stores always stood in the city centre and on the main streets and thoroughfares, or (as in the case of the railways) in the centre of the expanded urban areas that had now become necessary, usually above the pulled-down fortifications at the edges of former city centres.

Expediency before Beauty

What of the new public baths? These had neither the economic nor the symbolic significance of railway stations or arcades. They were frequently constructed on unattractive courtyard plots of land, thus preventing a representative, plastic articulation of the building (this is, at least, true of the early baths).

In the case of public baths, the general principle was that necessity and cleanliness come before beauty.[38] Today, looking at these pictures, this is difficult to believe for one could not completely renounce the architectonic and artistic articulation of these buildings, even if they are less pompous than railway stations, governmental buildings or department stores. The allotted budget was simply too small to allow this.

The greatest amount of money was used to construct entrance facades. The entire repertoire of Imperial building was employed: German and Italian Renaissance elements (Friedrichs Baths Baden-Baden), as well as fragments of additional styles. Today one feels obliged to define all this as eclecticism. The architects, however, only put into practice the existing architectural legacy.

The early baths (Kleine Flurstrasse, Wuppertal) were unplastered in the manner of schools or hospitals, while the use of decorative elements increased (the baths in Heidenheim). As a consequence of the general discussions about society and aesthetics in the latter part of the nineteenth century, filigree *Jugendstil* ornamentation was integrated into facades (Goseriede Baths, Hanover).

The design of the facade, already 'suffered' under the constraints of necessity. 'An important question remains the artistic stress on the entrance and foyer,' the Munich architect, Carl Hocheder, once stated before a professional public. 'Sadly, the most beautiful motif, the entrance hall one would wish to see in our baths is an element unsuitable for our climate. The draught-excluder, which is naturally much more sober, is therefore used as a substitute.'[39]

Sobriety was surely also applied to the many smaller areas, such as changing rooms, special steam and shower baths, rest areas and spaces for bathtubs. An example is the Vierordt Baths in Karlsruhe. It was opened on the 3 April 1873, shortly after the founding of the *Reich*. Following the School of Weinbrenner tradition in the best possible manner, a large, axially symmetric, H-shaped complex was originally constructed, crowned by a huge rotunda. When the Grand Duke of Baden suggested that a 'public bath' should be built, a thermal section was added. The rotunda enclosed a central building with steam and hot air baths lying behind it (in this case Roman-Irish and Russian). From the rotunda the visitor reached one of the two side buildings for male or female baths to the east and west.

'Cleansing' for reasons of hygiene, 'recuperation' in order to counteract the seventy-hour-week, but also 'healing' for medicinal reasons, were catchwords preceding the construction of the Vierordt Baths.[40] There were no swimming pools (as yet). Despite this 25,000 people visited the baths in 1897. After the turn of the century, demands for swimming pools became stronger. Finally, an extension was constructed, costing 597,000 Marks. This was initially a pool that destroyed the original symmetry of the building. (It was opened on 2 July 1900.)

While the swimming pool was later built over in Karlsruhe, in other cases it belonged to the concept of the building from the beginning. There were therefore usually two of these. In these cases, the side areas were constructed around the pools. Areas used by males and females, together, or by taking turns, were found in the middle axis of the bath. The areas separated according to sex were found on the outside. The pool's appearance resulted from a pettily exact concept of cleanliness. Ceramic tiles were naturally most welcome. Further extensions and the use of construction materials that were subject to a high degree of wear and tear because of dampness and warmth, changed in the course of time, as awareness of building materials and their characteristics increased. The iron and glass constructions, initially favoured (Charlottenburg Municipal Baths,

1899) in the construction of baths and elsewhere, were soon forbidden, due to great loss of heat and high corrosive damage, resulting from sweating. Open, wooden roof constructions were thus preferable to iron.

The vaulted, stuccoed roof could be constructed in a technically perfect manner only after about 1890 – the Municipal Baths in Breslau had one of the first roofs of this kind, with typical barrel vaulting, including side windows in the form of lunettes. Even later, it became possible to develop barrel vaulting with high side openings (Plärrer, Nuremberg). It was actually only after this time that pools in public baths 'no longer had a purely functional appearance.'[41] Before this, it had only been partially possible to hide a lack of space and boring ceiling decorations with wall paintings and reliefs (see Municipal Baths, Charlottenburg).

These gentle changes in style and decoration are an important aspect of the tiled world of public baths.

Müller's Public Baths –
the upbeat to a new era

A special role was assigned to one particular public baths. They were opened in 1901 and heralded a radical change in the development of public baths at the turn of the century. The architect, Carl Hocheder, had gathered much information about German public baths beforehand. He had travelled throughout Germany – from Berlin to Krefeld, from Hamburg to Stuttgart – researching meticulously. He suggested changes that were both surprising and of great consequence. He diverged 'from important aspects of the large baths developed in the nineteenth century'[42] and therefore gave further 'building of baths new impulses.'[43] As most of the baths illustrated in this book were constructed after 1901, special attention should be paid to Müller's Public Baths, which should be regarded as a prototype – leaving stylistic differences and their respective developments aside. Müller's Public Baths were, renovated in an exemplary fashion in 1984/1985 and now exist in prime condition – an accessible museum to the idea of the Public Bath that can be experienced at first hand.

The history of the building begins with a lengthy disagreement between the client and the architect. The client and donor was Johann Bernhard Müller (1821–1909). He was himself an architect and later, a civil servant, becoming wealthy after going into retirement. Müller's architectural ideas were those of early nineteenth-century Neo-Classicism. The architect, Carl Hocheder, had a picturesque style of building, which was shared by Camillo Sitte. Stated briefly, Hocheder triumphed over Müller and not only solved the 'task of designing the building functionally for the bather's needs' but also allowed the building to appear 'as if it was poured from a mould, along with the landscape and architectural surroundings.'[44] This was new. The prevailing, stark symmetry of baths was unsuitable. Due to sensible urban planning, the building led along the banks of the River Isar to the recently vacated Kohlinsel – not far from the German Museum, built a short while later. Organised in this way, the 4,000 square metres of usable floor space filled the Isar meadows like a foreign body. Hocheder made it appear as if the inner organisation was still based on separation of the sexes and that this was a multifunctional building. However, the new ensemble appeared loose, almost friendly. The foyer, vaulted towards the outside, was combined with the huge, elongated male swimming pool (a fact that should be seen within the context of the social significance of this style of building). The middle was dominated by a church tower (whose function was dispensing laundry). While the male pool appeared like a self-contained, heavy basilica, the female hall, placed in front, was designed as a small, fine, central building, with a flat cupola. The facades were structured without columns and pilasters, in a flat, almost modern, fashion. A tightrope act exists between the old and the new.

The Munich architectural historian, Winfried Nerdinger, summarised it as a 'mixture of *Jugendstil* elements, typical for Munich, to which Baroque and Neo-classical motifs are added.'[45]

As Carl Hocheder designed each square metre meticulously, he obviously contradicted the original 'building concept of necessity', dating from the initial phase of the German *Reich*. In the meantime the *Reich* had become richer, as had sections of its inhabitants, as is attested by the donation. Hocheder demonstrated all that the task of building a 'bath' entailed. The oval foyer is reminiscent of the inner courtyard of a Late Baroque castle, although the simple stucco and the absence of all ornamentation underlines its expedient. This hint of Neo-Baroque has given Hocheder a *Jugendstil* label – and the balconies growing out of the wall in the male hall appear to be formed out of wax by the Munich *Jugendstil* acrobat, August Endell. Hocheder himself stated, 'The artistic form should be influenced primarily by its usefulness and the construction of its frame-work. In the case of walls, at least, one could reject ornamental decoration completely and could limit this to the surface of the vaulting ...'[46]

A new age had indeed dawned. However, it would be misleading to attempt to under-stand Hocheder's architecture as already being functional. This could be claimed for a later generation of baths, for example, the Berlin-Mitte Municipal Baths by Heinrich Tessenow (1939) and the Stuttgart Haslach Municipal Baths (1929), where parabolic truss beams, consisting of iron and concrete, not only carry the ceiling, but also become the definitive elements of the design. The Baroque spirit, that of flowing space, dominates Müller's Public Baths more than the detail. Nonetheless, changes were in the air.

Towards new shores

Whether one is considering the Plärrer in Nuremberg, Berlin-Neukölln or Hamburg-Eppendorf (all finished in 1914), the development of these baths culminated in Müller's Public Baths. To some extent, the architecture took over stylistic and construction details. What was more important, however, was a similarity in ideas – the culmination point of the public baths as a building type was reached in the early twentieth century, surging on with reformatory movements beginning with the Arts and Crafts Movement, continuing with *Jugendstil* and later with the *Werkbund*. It is known that the models changed at the dawning of the century; the stylistic phraseology of the past disappeared. As Klaus-Jurgen Sembach stated, 'The historicism and the unfortunate taste of Wilhelm II appeared to have been overcome'.[47] This is hardly surprising, as the development of the modern industrial state did not allow for sentimentality. 'It had become a movement whose aims stretched beyond questions of style. It wished to make creativity more healthy and to cleanse the artistic spirit,'[48] concluded Fritz Schumacher, Director of Building in Hamburg at the time. Architecture became increasingly modern, but it was used in moderation, with only occasional overtures towards history.

The *Zweckbau* (expedient building) also changed appearance. Above all, this applied to factories, but also to hospitals and public buildings and naturally to the construction of baths. Public baths became symptomatic of a reformatory attitude during the beginnings of modernism. Architects had discovered both the type of space this could become and the qualities of new materials such as steel combined with concrete. Form and space took the place of ornamentation. Many baths now appeared to be as important as town halls. This was hardly surprising, as swimming pools were to be found under huge roofs because of their size.

Public baths were constructed well into the early years of World War 1. Most of the baths reproduced in this book date from this period. They were constructed thirty or forty years later than the older buildings and have therefore survived more successfully.

3. CONCLUSION: PUBLIC BATHS WITHOUT A FUTURE?

The development of public baths in the German *Kaiserreich* forms a special chapter in the culture of bathing. Baths constructed between 1871 and 1918 were influenced by the structural economy of the *Gründerzeit* but (following the motto, 'Wilhelm and the styles') experienced overblown historicism, until the whole was reformed by the periods of *Jugendstil* and the *Werkbund*. They both were, and are, sensitive gauges of style, fashion and the inner workings of the society of the time. This was formerly the case; although it is no longer so today.

It is true that many public baths survived the Imperial period and continued to serve their purpose over many years. In the following period, that of the Weimar Republic, the real problem arose – insufficient facilities available to the masses. Paradoxical as it sounds, part of the original function of public baths was brought into question by the aim of 'giving every person his apartment ration',[49] which naturally included a private bath. Nonetheless, they still existed and even the baths bombed in World War 11 were rebuilt in the homely style of the 1950s. People were grateful for every baths that had survived, and they were put to efficient use well into the 1970s, keeping up with the latest trends, both technically and aesthetically; sometimes though it was questionable whether the smooth, often harshly coloured, ceramic extensions were not rather unfortunate. The pictures in this volume speak for themselves.

Decline began with increased expenditure on power and personnel. Most apartments, in fact, had their own bathroom, and therefore new demands were made on public baths – the trend set by a new generation was initiated by the activity baths of the 1980s.[50] Several baths, such as the Holthusen Baths in Hamburg, kept up with these changes. Similarly, the huge bath in Eppendorf today has leisure landscapes of a new kind. This does not always go together well with the strict architectural and construction regulations but it provides amusement for visitors.

Other baths, such as Müller's Public Baths, were restored at great expense. This expenditure – about eight million marks with 134,000 yearly visitors in Munich[51] – was intimidating. At the Goseriede Baths in Hanover, nobody wanted to have a yearly deficit of 2.5 million marks, let alone commence restoration.[52] The Goseriede Baths was closed on 30 June 1982, seventy-five years after its opening. The pool was filled in with concrete.

Its future? Mosque, bowling alley, cultural centre, lecture hall, leisure bathing area, theatre, media centre, film school …?[53] Solutions are being sought in Hanover and elsewhere. What remains, however, is the fact that more and more baths (including those presented in this volume) are being closed. Perhaps even at this very moment …

1 *In den Tempeln der Badelust, Architekturen der Sinnlichkeit* (In the Joyful Temples of Bathing, Architectural Forms of Sensuality), Munich and Lucerne, 1986, p16. Living up to its title, this book explores this subject thoroughly in a lively and prosaic manner.

2 Dieter Leistner, Diploma at the University of Essen GHS, 1982, p6. Concerning photographic aspects of the series, see the essay by Hans-Eberhard Hess, 'Piercing Space'.

3 Johannes Roth, *Schwimmhallen und Badetempel* (Swimming Pools and Water Temples); an article in the *FAZ Magazin*, 21 May 1982.

4 Siegfried Giedion, *Wege in die Öffentlichkeit* (Paths towards the public eye), Essays and unpublished writings from the years 1926–1956, gta/Ammann, Zurich, 1987, p133ff.

5 'Weiterbauen', supplement of the *Schweizerische Bauzeitung* (Swiss Building Magazine), issue 3/1935, Zurich, 1935.

6 Ibid.

7 Horst Prignitz, *Wasserkur und Badelust* (Water Cures and Joys of Bathing), Koehler und Amelang, Leipzig, 1976, p27. This easily readable historical study may usefully be regarded as a 'bathing journey into the past'.

8 Ibid, p35.

9 Op cit, footnote 5.

10 Leonardo Benevolo, *Geschichte der Architektur des 19. Jahrhunderts und 20. Jahrhunderts*, Volume 1 (History of 19th and 20th Century Architecture); quoted from the paperback version, dtv, 5th edition, Munich, 1990, p90ff.

11 Ibid.

12 Barbara Hartmann, *Das Müller'sche Volksbad in München* (Müller's Public Baths), taduv Verlag, Munich, 1987, p5; this is a very important study of the development of public baths in Germany which reaches conclusions about the German hygiene movement and the development of public baths, far beyond the Munich example.

13 Ibid, p6.

14 Op cit, footnote 10, p90.

15 Hamburg, *Historisch-Topographische und Baugeschichtliche Mittheilungen von 1868* (Historical-topographical and architecturally historical

reports, 1868), reprint 1979, Hansa-Verlag, Hamburg, p97.

16 Ibid, p99.

17 Op cit, footnote 12, p8ff. This work cites further source material for this subject.

18 Oscar Lassar, *Volksbäder* (Public baths), Braunschweig, 1887, p12.

19 *Protokoll der Eröffnungssitzung der Deutschen Gesellschaft für Volksbäder* (Protocol of the Meeting opening the German Society for Public baths), 24 April 1899, published by the DGV, Volume I, Berlin, 1902, p40f.

20 Ibid, p42ff.

21 Ibid, p44ff

22 Ibid, Volume III, Berlin, 1906, p175ff.

23 Ibid, Volume II, Berlin, 1904, p212.

24 Op cit, footnote 10, p12ff.

25 Wolfgang R Krabbe, *Gesellschaftsveränderung durch Lebensreform. Strukturmerkmale einer sozial-reformerischen Bewegung in Deutschland der Industrialisierungsperiode* (Social Changes through Reforms in Lifestyle. Structural Characteristics of a Social Reformatory Movement in Germany's Period of Industrialisation), Göttingen, 1974.

26 *Veröffentlichungen der Deutschen Gesellschaft für Volksbäder* (Publications of the German Society for Public Baths), Göttingen, 1904, pp217–218.

27 Ibid, Volume IV, Berlin, 1907, p517. Reprint of an article in the monthly magazine, *Die Frau*.

28 *Berlin, Berlin,* exhibition catalogue, Nikolai Verlag, Berlin, 1987, p334.

29 Op cit, footnote 26, Volume III, p355.

30 Ibid, Volume III, p516ff.

31 Ibid, Volume III, p516ff.

32 Claude Mignot, *Architektur des 19. Jahrhunderts* (19th-Century Architecture), DVA, Stuttgart, 1983. Cf footnote 10, Benevolo. Both summaries of the history of architecture are recommended for those interested in understanding 19th-century architecture

33 Op cit, footnote 32, p12.

34 Ibid, p231.

35 Jean Dethier, *Die Welt der Bahnhöfe* (The Railway Station World), Exhibition catalogue, Berlin, 1981, p25.

36 JF Geist, *Passagen, ein Bautyp des 19. Jahr-*

hunders (Arcades, a 19th-Century Building Type), Prestel, Munich, 1979, p223ff.

37 Op cit, footnote 35. p9.

38 Op cit, footnote 12, p15ff.

39 Op cit, footnote 26, Volume III, p252ff.

40 *Hektographierte Informationen des Sport- und Bäderamts Karlsruhe* (Hectographed Information of the Sports and Bathing Department in Karlsruhe).

41 Op cit, footnote 12, p18.

42 Ibid, p99.

43 Ibid, p101.

44 Ibid, p72ff.

45 Winifried Nerdinger, 'Neue Strömungen und Reformen zwischen Jugendstil und Neue Sachlich-keit' (New Movements and Reforms between Jugendstil and Neue Sachlichkeit) in: *Bauen in München 1890–1950,* Munich, 1980, p41ff.

46 Carl Hocheder, in: *Der Baumeister* (The Master Builder) 3/1905, Munich, p103.

47 Klaus-Jurgen Sembach, in: *1910, Halbzeit der Moderne* (Half-time of Modernism) exhibition catalogue, Hatje Verlag, 1992: p9ff. This essay is recommended for a greater understanding of this time.

48 Fritz Schumacher, *Stufen des Lebens* (Stages in Life), DVA, Stuttgart, 1983, p14.

49 Lieselotte Ungers, *Die Suche nach einer neuen Wohnform, Siedlungen der zwanziger Jahre* (Searching for a New Form for Living, Housing Developments in the Twenties), DVA, Stuttgart, 1983, p14.

50 Gerd Meyhöfer, *Das Baden ist des Deutschen Lust* (Bathing is a German's Delight), Verlag Budde, Herne, 1993.

51 Klaus Dieter Weiss, 'Schlag ins Wasser, der Pflege-fall Goseriedebad Hanover' (Falling into the Water – The Sad Case of the Goseriedebad in Hanover), in *Bauwelt* 23/1991, p1162ff.

52 Ibid.

53 Compare footnote 51.

VIERORDT BATHS, KARLSRUHE, 1873

The architect, Josef Durm, remained close
to the tradition of the architectural school
founded by the Neo-Classicist, Karl-Fried-
rich Weinbrenner. Durm therefore designed a sober, axially symmetrical, shaped
complex, stylistically indebted to examples
found in the Renaissance. Early Imperial
German baths rarely included a swimming
pool; here in Karlsruhe it was extended at
the turn of the century (see also p18)

Swimming pool with overhead lighting

FRIEDRICHS BATHS,
BADEN-BADEN, 1877

The Friedrichs Baths, erected by Court architect, Carl von Dernfeld – incorporating Renaissance elements – does not strictly belong to the category of public bathing facilities, for it is a prototype of the exclusive spas of the time. One should note, however, that the complex with its succession of cleansing, thermal, bubbling and steam baths is reminiscent of traditional Roman baths.

Thermal exercise pool under the dome, the centrepiece of the building

Thermal plunge-bath

Thermal bubble pool

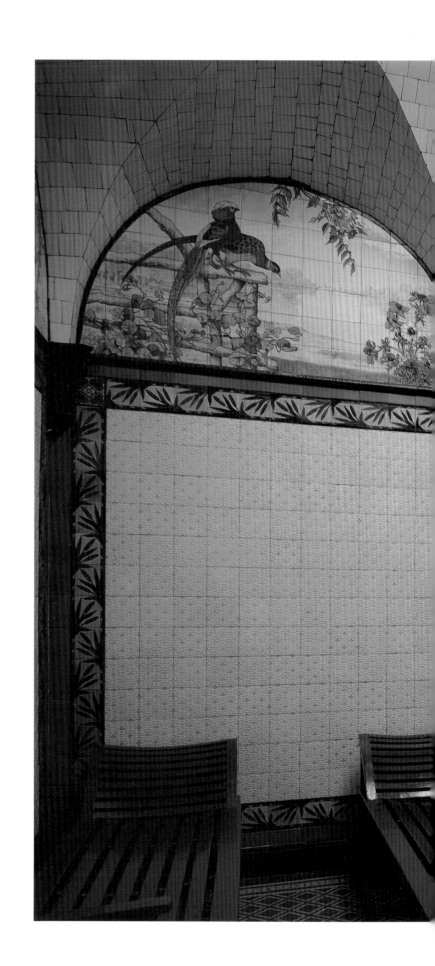

Wall mosaic in the hot air room

THEDESTRASSE,
HAMBURG-ALTONA, 1881

Originally built of yellow clinker brick,
modesty was the main characteristic of
these small working class baths (architect:
A Petersen). The pool consisted of only
150 cubic metres. The groundplan was
distinctive: the baths followed the direc-
tion of an existing street, bending in a
V-shape. Separate male and female baths
were located here. The small, closed swimming pool was placed in the protected
courtyard. The baths have been closed for
years, however, they are used occasionally
for a variety of activities.

KLEINE FLURSTRASSE,
WUPPERTAL, 1882

The small bathing complex in the Barmer Flurstrasse has a front facade made of unfired bricks as was customary during the *Gründerzeit* (they were also used for sewers and factories at this time). The interior was designed in a highly discreet manner, according to the guiding principle, 'necessity comes before beauty'. The baths have been classified as a historical monument. As they are to be closed in the near future, attempts are being made to find an appropriate new purpose.

Symmetrical stairway leading to the upper gallery

35

Two-storey changing area, frontal view

Ladies' pool, detail

HALLEN BATHS GERA, 1892

This complex is one of the oldest sur-
viving bathing facilities in the former
East Germany. Its atmosphere is tasteful,
almost intimate. This is a result of the flat
roof construction, for overhead lighting
was not yet customary at this time. The
Hallen Baths are still in use.

Swimming pool

EBERTPLATZ MUNICIPAL BATHS, OBERHAUSEN, 1895

Although the mines and iron works of the Ruhr area had their own baths (eg washing cubicles), it was felt necessary to construct public bathing facilities in this area of the *Reich* because it had the highest population. The baths at Oberhausen possess one of the earliest examples of a circular roof above a swimming pool with overhead lighting. They have since been closed and reconstructed.

Swimming pool with overhead lighting

CHARLOTTENBURG
MUNICIPAL BATHS, BERLIN, 1899

This is one of the few baths still in existence with a glass and iron roof construction over the swimming pool. The wall decoration on the main wall masks the distinct impression that the building resembles a factory. The baths in Charlottenburg were renovated and extended several times. (Design: Municipal Planner, Paul Bratring, with Municipal Inspector of Buildings, Peters; cost: c512,000 Goldmarks.)

Swimming pool with a glass and iron roof

DESSAU MUNICIPAL BATHS, 1900

At the turn of the century, a swimming
pool was constructed in the city that was
later to be famous for the Bauhaus. Con-
ceivably the sober building style predates
the ideas of Walter Gropius. According
to the standards of the time, the ceiling
of the swimming pool was kept to a functional, low height.

Swimming pool, photographed in 1993

PRENZLAUER BERG
MUNICIPAL BATHS, BERLIN, 1900

The municipal baths of the Prenzlauer
Berg area are no longer in use. They were
opened in the year 1900 and took on the
function of baths in an urban area of the
capital. It was part of the progressive
bathing concept in Berlin that wished to
accommodate above all the thickly popu-
lated inner city areas. The baths are to be
renovated and reopened.

Swimming pool that is no longer in use, photographed in 1993

POTSDAM PUBLIC BATHS, 1900

The circular hall in this example conveys
a ceremonial impression and therefore
blends with the splendour of the former
Prussian Versailles. By contrast, the struc-
ture of the interior is in a highly sober
style. The circular motif is adopted by
the windows and arcades. The baths have
been closed.

Swimming pool, 1993

MÜLLER'S PUBLIC BATHS,
MUNICH, 1901

The Munich complex, which is located
beside the River Isar, was built in 1901 at
the height of the public bath movement.
Its unusual sensitively-structured architecture and successful relationship with the
urban site make it exceptional. It was an
example for baths that followed. (Architect: Professor Carl Hocheder [see p19ff].)

Former male swimming pool, end wall with clock, photographed in 1982

Former male swimming pool,
overall view, photographed in 1982

Former female pool, photographed in 1982

Fountain detail

COVERED BATHS, WUPPERTAL, 1902

The municipal baths on the Friedrich-
Engels-Allee in Wuppertal are still in use,
although their future is uncertain. The
roof construction, typical for baths dating
from the beginning of the twentieth century, is particularly well developed. Semi-
circular window openings are cut into the
vaulted, stuccoed roof. They provide clear
light, that is not unpleasantly bright.

GOSERIEDE BATHS, HANOVER, 1903

The Goseriede Baths are one of the most famous baths. They formerly included three swimming pools, forty tubs, a steam and hot air bath and a dog bath in the cellar! The architect, Carl Wolff, the director of Municipal Planning in Hanover at this time, could only partially realise his characteristic *Jugendstil* ornamentation for budgetary reasons. The entrance hall was badly damaged in World War II and a simpler version was rebuilt in the style of the Fifties. The baths have since been closed.

Female pool, extensively restructured in the post-war period,
eg a new false ceiling was constructed

LEONARDSBERG MUNICIPAL BATHS, AUGSBURG, 1903

A stroke of luck made a 'second lease of life' possible for one of the most beautiful public baths in Bavaria (architects: Municipal Building Department and the architect, Stein).

The former Bavarian Prime Minister, Franz Josef Strauss – on the occasion of Augsberg's 2000th anniversary in 1985 – promised state funds if the facility, that was then closed, was reopened. Because of this, since 1992, the Municipal Baths, with two swimming pools and numerous *Jugendstil* fragments in the sauna areas, have been restored to their former glory.

Swimming pool in the process of being closed down, 1984

HEIDENHEIM PUBLIC BATHS, 1906

Heidenheim was influenced by Müller's Public Baths. The design was by the Stuttgart architect, Philipp Jakob Manz, although in comparison with the example in Munich the 'space was regulated and simplified to a large extent'. The *Jugendstil* building, classified as a historical monument, was closed in 1988, due to strong competition from a leisure pool. It is presently an art gallery.

Jugendstil changing area

LUDWIGSBURG
MUNICIPAL BATHS, 1907

This bathing facility was constructed
beside a school in 1907 (architects:
P Schmohl and G Staehlin). The extremely
high roof construction is striking, as is the
effective lighting in the hall, due to the
large window areas in the roof. It is used
today as a warm bath with a water temperature of twenty-nine degrees Celsius.

Swimming pool, overall view

JENA PUBLIC BATHS, 1907/08

The high hall of the baths has a very special atmosphere. The elongated applications on the capitals of the columns in the lower gallery are particularly noteworthy. Semi-circular windows are positioned above the gallery, providing dynamic overhead lighting.

STEGLITZ MUNICIPAL BATHS, BERLIN, 1908

The municipal baths in Steglitz included
a Roman-Irish bath, as was usual at the
beginning of the century. There was also
a library. The complex design of the end
wall is a striking feature of this pool. The
semi-circular rotunda creates a ceremonial
atmosphere, similar to that found in
churches. (Architects: Blunck and Münzen-
berger.)

ELISABETH HALL, AACHEN, 1911

With inauspicious beginnings, the baths,
which opened in June 1911, were closed
until February 1912 due to a lack of water.
The architect and Municipal Commissioner
of Buildings, Laurent, had to blend the
narrow facade of the huge complex – de-
corated with gold – into a narrow plot
of remaining land. Two swimming pools,
one behind the other, therefore created
the unusual ground plan. The building
was renovated in 1975/76 and is still in
use today.

Aesculapius fountain in the former male swimming pool

Late *Jugendstil* – changing areas with authentic mirrors and clothes racks

Former male swimming pool, overall view

Former female swimming pool,
frontal view

NEPTUN BATHS, COLOGNE, 1912

In the first decade of the century the baths
were removed to the suburbs because the
cities had grown to such an extent that
the inner city baths could no longer accommodate the growing population. The
Neptun Baths in the Ehrenfeld area (architect: Kleefisch) are the first example of
'suburban baths' in Cologne (compare
also the Deutz-Kalk baths). There is a small
pool, measuring 21×9.5 metres, twenty-
eight tubs and twenty-seven showers etc.
The strong colours of the tiles in the hall
are striking. The Neptun Baths have been
classified as a historic building and are
now in full use.

Entrance hall

77

Swimming pool

PUBLIC BATHS, PLÄRRER SQUARE, NUREMBERG, 1913

It can be assumed that since Munich is nearby, Müller's Public Baths followed the Plärrer example. Similar facilities are in evidence (three swimming pools, eight tubs and twenty-four showers, as well as steam and hot air baths). The construction of the Nuremberg baths is, however, more modern. The imposing vaulting of the roof and the swimming pools is made of iron and steel. These pools stand freely on columns. (Architects: Municipal Building Department, headed by Carl Weber; planning: Chief Engineer, Kufner.) Two halls were closed down in 1992; the third is only open on an hourly basis.

Large swimming pool, end wall, photographed in 1980

Female swimming pool with architectural extensions,
dating from the post-war period

Large male swimming pool
(photographed in 1993, after it had been closed down)

Former small male swimming pool –
Armenhalle or 'pool for the poor',
photographed in 1980

DEUTZ-KALKER BATHS, COLOGNE, 1913

These were constructed in 1913, the year preceding the war at a cost of approximately 751,000 Goldmarks. They were badly damaged in World War II, were classified as a historical monument and have acted as a provisional thermal bath since 1989. For this reason, thermal water is supplied by lorry from the nearby Rheinpark spas. The pool appears sober and strict compared with the others, for the vaulted roof found elsewhere was rejected in this case. (Cf the Neptun Baths.)

Swimming pool with flat roof and
overhead lighting from the side

HOLTHUSEN BATHS, HAMBURG-EPPENDORF, 1914

These facilities are amongst those complexes opened shortly before the war. They possess a clear architectural language in the spirit of 'form before ornamentation'. Parts of the Holthusen Baths have been enlarged and rebuilt since 1985 to form a leisure bath. Included are a thermal bath, a wave bath as well as additional attractions such as waterfalls.

Changing area before restoration, photographed in 1982

Swimming pool

HALLE MUNICIPAL BATHS, 1914

These baths in the city on the River Saale were completed shortly after World War I, reflecting the robust architectural character of the time. The baths urgently need repairs but in the meantime have lost none of their charm. Halle indicates that already at this time a great deal of attention was paid to subsidiary rooms and activities.

Sauna, as it was in 1993

Female swimming pool

NEUKÖLLN MUNICIPAL BATHS, BERLIN, 1914

The local baths in Berlin-Neukölln appear as dignified as a Roman model. This is no coincidence, as the former Municipal Commissioner of Buildings, Reinhold Kiehl, had previously made a careful study of Roman examples. Kiehl designed a generous area for a combination of sports, hygienic, medicinal and spiritual facilities (a library was formerly included). He therefore advanced the development of public bathing facilities considerably. The pool was extensively renovated and redesigned in 1984. All photographs were taken in 1993.

Sauna, overall view

Large swimming pool (former male pool)

Small swimming pool (former female pool)

Large swimming pool, frontal view, 1993

LEIPZIG MUNICIPAL BATHS, 1916

The construction of these metropolitan
baths was begun in March, 1913. As a
result of the war, they could only be put
into operation three years later. The complex includes several swimming pools and
numerous additional areas. These were all
extensively reconstructed from 1987 to
1989. During reconstruction, particular
emphasis was placed on recreating Islamic
decorative elements in the sauna area.
(Architect: Otto Wilhelm Scharenberg,
Municipal Commissioner of Buildings.)

Large swimming pool

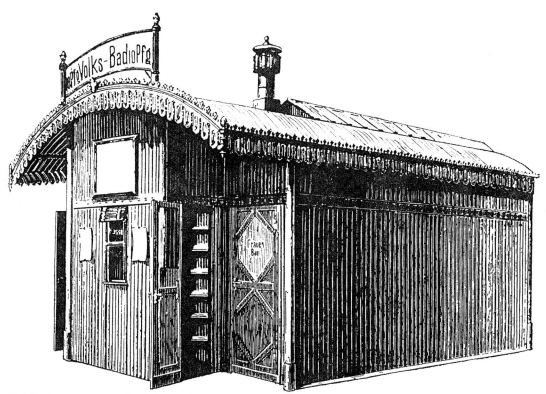

Public baths – standard type

Schweinemarkt baths, Hamburg

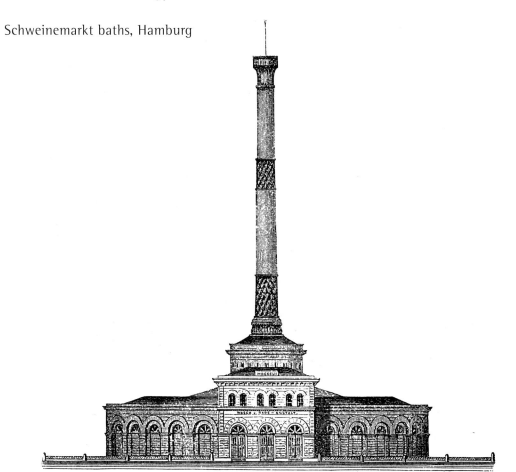

Vierordt Baths, drawing of outside view

Vierordt Baths, ground plan

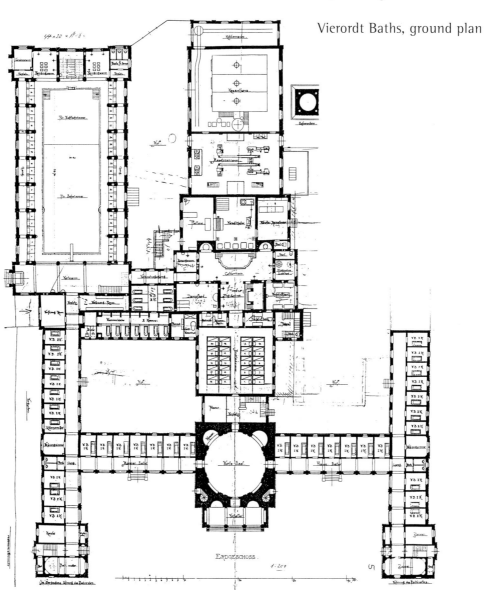

ERDGESCHOSS.

109

Kleine Flurstraße, view from the outside

Müller's Public Baths, view

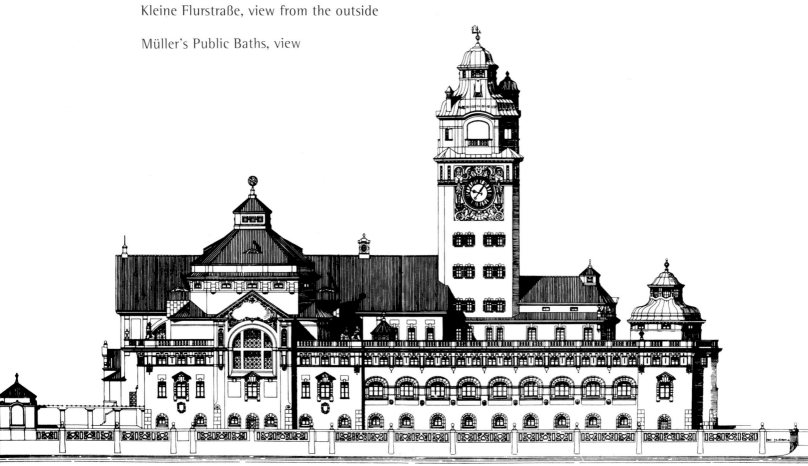

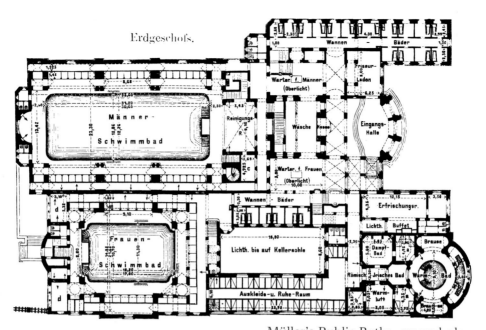

Müller's Public Baths, ground plan

Goseriede Baths, photographed from the outside

111

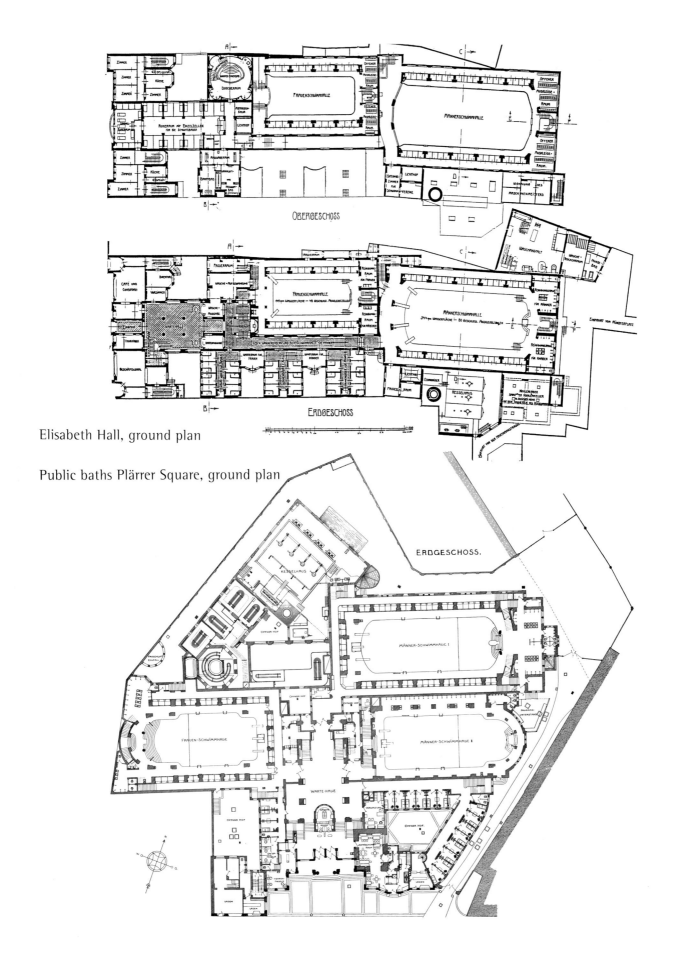

Elisabeth Hall, ground plan

Public baths Plärrer Square, ground plan